I Stumbled to Rise in Purpose: Ronjeanna's Encouraging Thoughts

By Ronjeanna Harris

ISBN: 978-1-7358024-3-5

Front cover image by Towanda V. Little
Edited by Katherine A. Young (www.katherineayoung.com)

Printed by Write It Out Publishing, Inc. in the United States of America.

Write It Out Publishing LLC
Virginia Beach, Virginia
writeitout@gmail.com
757-276-3640

www.justjeannas.com

Dedications

First, all honor to God & my Lord and Savior, Jesus Christ, for guiding me in this assignment.

My husband Floyd Harris

My children: Kerra Harris, Briona Harmon, Kestasia Smith, Jalon Harmon, Jy'Asia Smith, Raniya Harris, & JeanMa's Baby Ellie

My parents: Deacon Ronnie Smith & Minister Barbara Smith

My spiritual leaders: Apostle Dannie R. Ducksworth & Pastor Elder Rebecca G. Ducksworth

My Mentors: Jeanita Castille & Dr. Dionne Gibbs

To everyone that has supported, sown, and encouraged in any way during this journey so far: A BIG THANK YOU.

Introduction

Learning to look through God's eyes is easier said than done. We find ourselves talking great and sounding good. However, we never really tap into pure trust in God to perform using our purposed passion. Unsure thoughts like that will easily dwindle your journey to your purpose and destiny. It is important to always stay focused spiritually, mentally, and physically. I can attest to this statement because in my immature state, I had planned to write this book around 2007-2008, but I never completed it. If I would have, my message would not have been as clear because I was not walking completely in my purpose; I would have released immature thoughts and emotions into the atmosphere for millions to read, leading to an unfortunate and ineffective purpose. God confirmed that the time was NOW to share my story. My goal is to encourage people, young and old, around the world from all walks of life. I pray my book blesses you spiritually and naturally.

Sincerely,

Ronjeanna

June 24, 2019

Table of Contents

Thoughts on Purpose

I would often go back and forth about this word. Let us talk about it.

First, let us understand the definition of *purpose*:

Per the dictionary, the noun definition states: "the reason which something is done or created or for which something exists."

The verb definition states: "have as one's intention or objective."

When you focus on purpose, passion should also come to mind. In my opinion, they go hand in hand. There is an unexplainable drive in you that ignites when you operate fully in the purpose God predestined for you. Do you feel that now with what you do? If not, seek God for direction and wait for his answer.

Having passion about or for anything you do is important because it determines:

*Your delivery: How is understanding established?

> Present in a way that the concept is captured.

* Your effectiveness: Did it fulfill the purpose intended?

> Make sure it is realistic for others to understand the concept to obtain conquering the intended purpose.

*Your longevity: Will this help for future encounters?

We must not consider ourselves when operating in our purpose. Yes, put your heart and soul into what you do. But focus on limiting your emotions. Why? If not, it then becomes about you and does not serve the full purpose the way God wanted you to deliver the message. From experience, I have learned the hard way. It is important to keep your eyes on God. Your life depends on it as well as the lives of the ones God has assigned to you for the purpose of witnessing.

I have grown to examine my approach towards people and situations. The reason may be right, but was the timing? And did you deliver it the way God wanted it delivered? See, we must do it God's way if we want to be effective, right? People are often prone to receive things the wrong way; I know I have been guilty of doing the same. Everyone is not open-minded to receive if the approach is perceived as distasteful.

Now let me also mention this: you will not reach everyone but be obedient to God's instructions. Through self-examination, I had to get to the ugly core of myself and deal with sensitive issues to understand my purpose. My sensitive issues surrounded the "why is" and "how comes." The gut-wrenching truth of myself is what I am talking about. All our tests and trials are for someone else who may experience the same situations, and we need to be prepared to tell them how to effectively overcome.

When you are delivering your message, be mindful to share with kindness and compassion. Sometimes we abuse the "keep it real" lingo, especially when dealing with people that are already at their breaking point. "Keeping it real" may be a realistic way to give it to them straight, so they will be able to receive it and apply the advice better. But it may not always be the best method. I remember how I would act when something was said to me when someone was trying to "keep it real" and I clearly did not want to hear or receive not one word. A rage would build up inside of me because my mind would be so cloudy, preventing me from digesting the truth. So, it is best to use wisdom and share the truth with love and kindness.

Using situations as an excuse to not operate in my truth, purpose, or passion, I stayed in denial for so long. God literally had to position the death angels at my door to really open my eyes. I was becoming reckless trying to justify my behavior while falling deeper into the pit that I created by partying and heavily drinking. I mean the mass consumption of alcohol I was taking in was unreal. Many people did not see that part. Self-inflicted from my actions of being reckless with alcohol, I began having heart issues. The scripture that mentions you will receive a warning before destruction, totally applied to my life at this time because I came awfully close more than once—but God.

How Spiritual Attacks Influence Natural Components of You

During my denial stage I mentioned earlier, I developed heart issues. In 2017, I was diagnosed with Supraventricular Tachycardia (SVT). God broke down what it meant for my life to me in the beginning of this month of June and I began to write:

SVT: rapid heartbeat

My heart was beating for more than one person. In my case, ungodly spirits were starting to attach to me, causing unnatural attacks of my body. My heart vessel and chamber were being stretched beyond normal capacity. This portal was open because I got out of the will of God. Whew chile! It's deep, but real. This is an example of not being in your purpose that God has for you.

Understand that some tests and trials are a part of your purpose. But in my situation, my issues were self-inflicted because I was running from my purpose.

Keys to Understand and Remember:

1. Know what your purpose is

2. Understand your purpose

3. Follow the instructions of your purpose

4. Operate in your purpose

5. Live your purpose

6. Manifest effectiveness in your purpose

7. Stay in obedience to your purpose

It's vital you conduct your own soul-searching to get the appropriate answers designed for you. Pray, seek God, read the Bible, and have the right spiritually assigned guidance that's kingdom minded.

Notes/Thoughts:_____

_____

_____

_____

_____

_____

_____

_____

_____

_____

_____

_____

_____

_____

_____

_____

Conquering Purpose

Powerful stories in the bible such as Noah and the Ark; the story of Abraham; the story of Moses: the story of Esther, and so many more allowed God to use them for purpose has always helped me to see that I, too, can be used for purpose. These individuals served their purpose the way God instructed. They may not have been perfect, but they were obedient in pursuing purpose.

Sharing the Word of God has been delivered in so many ways for years. There is not just one way to share and minister. Your method of delivery is just right for the right people to receive your purpose you are sharing.

Along with purpose, humility is needed. I Peter 5:6 says to *"Humble yourselves therefore under the mighty hand of God, that he may exalt you in due time."* God's timing is important. Having purpose is great, but it must be fulfilled in the right season, meeting a need in order for it to be effective. Humility helps you stay level-headed. We do not want a "big head" mindset because when that happens, we take God out of the picture and then all of the focus is on you. Then your purpose becomes contaminated, thus affecting your attempts to speak life into others. That can be extremely dangerous if not recognized right away. I just love how God amazingly reveals revelations to His children, which we can grasp to help us grow into our purpose. We must allow God's will for our lives—although He does give us free will, but we know God's will for our life is effective and has worth. Once I stopped running and decided to allow God's will for my life, my purpose started to make sense to me, even past experiences from my youth. There was purpose in watching my mother suffer with depression, having nervous breakdowns, and dealing with PTSD. Becoming a mother at the age of sixteen was also a part of my purpose. LIFE plays a big part in growing effectively in your purpose.

Once you accept your purpose, you must seek to understand why things happened the way it did. What could I have done differently? What signals did I miss? What made me behave in such a manner? Allow God to give you understanding, and do not make your own analysis. *Proverbs 3:5-6* says *"Trust in the Lord with all thine heart and lean not unto thine own understanding. In all thy ways acknowledge him, and he shall direct thy paths."* Plain and simple, these are clear instructions.

Let's now focus on how to obtain your knowledge of your purpose. In your purpose, you are humble. You must go out and do the work. Yep, that is right: work your purpose. The people are not going to come running to you. That would be too easy. We want to then tap into our gift of discernment and discerning of spirits to connect to the right people. Remember God has people and resources assigned specifically to you. So now we must always be prayerful to God for direction. Asking the Lord to order your steps to prevent you from taking a right when God really wanted you to take a left is important. Reflecting on my own life experiences of operating in pure disobedience, I remember how each act put me on an unnecessary merry-go-round in life. Do not assume I have it all together now—I do not. But what I do have now is God as my director instead of trying to do everything myself. I am now trying to avoid self-inflicted hardships. Just stick to God's will; His way is the only way to a successful end. God is so awesome. Being obedient is all a part of being effective in your purpose. Moving with the flow of God's divine purpose for you will lead you to your destination of greatness. Again, always seek Him. Stay motivated with a positive mindset. Always speak life into your purpose.

Some helpful ways to stay on track

1. Get clear instructions from God by praying and reading the bible for revelation.

2. Write and repeat positive affirmations every day by reading books and articles, as well as listening to positive channels to build your mind.

3. Stay clear of negative influences by conditioning your mind through the use of meditation, prayer, and worship music before starting your day.

4. Stay focused by realizing intentionally speaking positive over yourself is a lifestyle change.

5. Keep moving by staying on track through consistency.

6. Never give up: your purpose is bigger than you; someone's destiny is depending on your decision to continue in purpose.

7. Learn from tests and trials to be better; it is always a lesson for your blessing.

Notes/thoughts:_____

_____

_____

_____

_____

_____

_____

_____

_____

_____

_____

_____

_____

_____

_____

Thoughts of Passion

Along with purpose, passion is a very deep and creative word in its own right. It is a deep inner tugging of one's heart's desire for a craft. It is something you cannot stop thinking about. Ideas pour in and even on the roughest day, you still find joy doing that work or craft because it is a part of your passion.

The dictionary definition of *passion* states:

> *"Passion is a feeling of intense enthusiasm towards or compelling desire for someone or something."*

This is key to what you do in life. You must have an inner God-given passion with what you do. The success and effectiveness of the outcome depends on it. It may not always be easy, but it will be accomplished for great delivery.

So, ask yourself, "Is this my passion?" in relation to that job, business, or organization. Now understand we must use wisdom and do what we need to do to earn income to take care of our households. But when God clears the path for you to go forth to leave a certain chapter in your life, He will provide resources and supply every need. Whatever you find your truth to be in the answer you receive, pray about it. Then allow God to direct you. Don't rush: you do not want to move in the wrong timing. Remember: we want to avoid self-inflicting situations.

Pursuing passion can be hard because it means so much to you, that you sometimes will overthink the simplest things. You end up over-evaluating which decisions are good or bad. Most times, the still voice inside of you has already told you what and how to master working your passion. You have to be still enough to listen. This is why it is vital for you to start your day with God asking the Holy Spirit to lead and guide you.

Passion will require you to take risks but remember that you are not doing this on your own. You have God's guidance. When you are utilizing your passion, you are truly activating your faith walk. And I know all too well about this! It literally takes you out of self because everything is at the command of God's instructions. And if this is not your mindset, then prayer and reading your Word (the bible) will help get you on track. Understand this: you can listen to people all day, but if something does not ignite inside to push you to use your passion under the will of God's purpose for you, all that talking is falling on your deaf ears. *Purpose* and *passion* connect for your life. Sometimes, passion is not knowing what is going to happen next. You just have to be in position to move. It's not about the perfect time or the so-called perfect amount of money. Living in the will of God by using your purpose and passion is having the right posture for supernatural balance to go forth. See, when you have that, nothing can easily get you off course of your path. When it is the roughest day you feel imaginable, you can still overcome and be great in your passion. God must assign you your passion; you cannot just go find something or take on any type of passion. It must be yours. You can only be effective is by following in your passion. Passion helps you establish stability and standards. Passion is something you deeply love to do, so you are going to be careful with it.

Passion is so broad. It just explains so many points of your life that did not make sense. Think about it: look back at some of your life experiences and write your thoughts on how it helped you in some way.

Key points

1. Work your assigned passion. Do what you were created to do.
2. Understand your passion. Seek guidance through prayer and reading the Word of God.

3. Have balance doing your passion. Fulfill your assignment without neglecting everyday life duties.

4. Make sure your passion has a positive effect. Be intentional, effective, operating in purpose.

Notes/thoughts:_____

_____

_____

_____

_____

_____

_____

_____

_____

_____

_____

_____

_____

_____

_____

_____

Passion opens so many awesome doors if you allow it. It creates an inner drive to willingly promote greatness for others by doing what you love. In order to have passion, you need to be flowing in your God-given passion in order to be effective. Can you get back in to reach that inner thrive God has embedded in you? Sure, you can, but deep down, you have to sincerely want it. That is the key, remember you have choices. God gives you free will. The decision to use your purpose and passion is yours.

So, the question I want to pose for you is this: are you operating in passion today? If you are—awesome. If not, seek God for the answers you need to proceed to operate in passion if your heart desires it, God will give it to you. Psalms 37: 4 says *"Delight yourself in the Lord, and he will give you the desires of your heart."* This scripture clearly shows that you must want it. Starting today, you will operate in life with passion if you desire it and seek to willingly use it.

Trusting the Process for God's Plan and Will for Your Life is Important

So, let us talk a little bit about *trust*.

The definition of *trust* is to have a *"firm belief in the reliability, truth, ability, or strength of someone or something."*

Wow, you must have belief in something or someone. That means you must believe in God during your process (God is the someone). And you must believe in your purpose (purpose is the something). This also means giving God full control without your assistance. Allow God to prepare the way. Most times, it is easier said than done. Operating in your passion has a cost, even though you are doing what you absolutely love. Rainbows will not be in the sky all the time. Why? Because when you are creating healing and deliverance for yourself and others to recognize their purpose and passion, the enemy does not like that. Satan's camp is being minimized and God's kingdom is being enlarged. You must have a "get it done" type of mindset when you are operating in passion. This inner desire provokes you to give it your all. This means pushing beyond your max to accomplish something meaningful. People's lives will never be the same because you decided to take that extra push. Isn't that amazing?

Walking in manifestation is flourished through operating in purpose. Destiny takes the wheel. Passion aligns every step. Never let what you see in your current situation cost you to miss your arrival. Always pray, read your bible, and only entertain positive intentions for your life. Now your journey may not be easy, but if you stay determined and consistent, it will be worth it. You can do all things through Jesus Christ who strengthens you. The bible says so. Always research vital information for yourself. Only take God at His word. Even if someone is praying for you, you want to go to God for yourself to make sure it is legit. This is particularly important. Be open to change. Most times, the very thing that God has assigned for our lives is where we are most uncomfortable operating. Always be kind, teachable, and a good listener. You demonstrate great wisdom in those areas if you follow God's way.

Always quote and declare positive affirmations over every aspect of your life. No matter what you do, make sure you do it in your assigned purpose, allowing God to map out the guidelines for your life. Stay dedicated. Build the type of strength and faith that when times get shaky or unsure, you can encourage yourself. Do not wait on people to celebrate you. Listen: if God gives you an assignment, He will provide you with everything to complete it. In addition, do not let anything hinder your assigned purpose. Sometimes, you may have to correct past situations in order to move forward. Just pray for God to direct you. Again, do not be in a rush. When the time is right, everything you believe God for will happen.

Obedience in purpose will cause you to do what is unpopular nor trendy. You may not be understood, and that is perfectly okay. Just make sure you are seeking God and waiting for instructions from Him. Listening is particularly important. Having a keen ear to fully know about your assignment is very important.

Who would have thought purpose would win through little ole me, a girl from the Eastern Shore who had all odds against her? All glory to God!

This is the season to emerge into what God has created us to do. We are divinely assigned with purpose. We are to help others through our life journeys. It will never be easy; however, Heaven's reward is great. Hearing God strategically—especially with an assignment that will move with major impact on the lives of those it touches, is important. One thing that is important to practice is to not have a one-sided walk in your purpose. Your mindset must be examined frequently to not damage someone you are supposed to be helping. Be so focused that every resource God sends you fulfills their entire purpose for you to soar. Pray and acknowledge the level of impact you're supposed to make and seek God's guidance in it. Wherever your purpose and passion lead you, be it locally in the community, nationally, internationally, or perhaps a combination of all locales, be sure to serve in the assigned area created just for you.

I was told by an awesome and powerful Woman of God to not hold back and say what God gives me. My purpose awakened even more. I wanted to see people be free and find their true selves. I yearned for the feeling to impact more lives to commit to God and flow in their God-given purpose. Hidden fears that I thought I was delivered from at that point had to die. Spiritual boldness was igniting with the hope of encouragement to push and uplift others. God's direction is the only way to not sabotage your purpose. The guidance of God is emergent in this day and time. Everything may not make sense all at once, but obedience is mandatory. Listen, and grow in God. He will develop you in purpose. Let God breathe His purpose for you into you.

I ran and ran for years; my goodness—it almost cost me my life. Purpose will remind you that it is not about you. God gave me several chances. When I received the final call, instead of running, I thanked God I had a sound mind to say I was going to do right and follow Him. A transition occurred in my life where I started looking and feeling different. I began going through a process of seasons of shifting and renewing. Cleansing and healing had to take place God's way. We must not as believers participate in practices such as smudging, tapping bowls, or even talking to ancestors. See, the problem with many of us is that we sometimes dabble in things during our development stage, which then opens up realms that delay us flowing in our full potential effectively. I made a declaration that compromising my walk with God would never be a forethought when operating in any area of my life. I am sold out to God. Kingdom building for me is mandatory. I listened to God. I made sure to stay connected with my spiritual leaders to stay covered.

I remain teachable. Prayer is important because it is another preventative measure to avoid destruction. Purpose makes you take a stand when nobody else will and when it feels like the whole world is against you. Stand anyway! Have a zeal for the cause that gives excitement to your inner man.

Purpose requires stretching. Dedication and consistency are important in achieving your assigned purpose that God has for you. We must apply the word of God to your purpose. Do not compromise your assigned purpose for convenience. Purpose will always supersede the expectation of man. Whatever your purpose is, God will give you gems to be successful in it. Never allow obstacles stop you from moving forward. Give purpose all that you have and then some. The road and journey will not be easy, but think of how many lives you can help though your assigned purpose. Something I wrote to myself in 2018 to encourage myself and I want to share it to encourage you: "If you never get any recognition, as long as you please God, that's satisfaction enough."

God often speaks this in my spirit: "It doesn't make a difference if it doesn't make an impact in purpose." Leap into faith through God's direction. Take good risks. Do not be fearful of the unknown because that chance may not come by again. One thing that really moves me and I hope it does the same for others, is that I love seeing people win. I mean really winning, conquering, and finding their true self in purpose. I love encouraging others. I love seeing people overcoming obstacles. I am charged through my mandate to let people know and understand purpose in the simplest terms.

If you read this and feel you need to go back to the drawing board, that is fine. As long as you reevaluate your purpose and continue to move forward. One scripture that I love is Jeremiah 1:5a because it speaks volumes about purpose. Jeremiah 1:5a says *"Before I formed thee in the belly, I knew thee…"* God already knew us and every step we would take: mistakes and all. But guess what? We still have assigned purpose. If you read this book this far, you must have a desire to operate in your purpose. Did you get up thinking you could change the world in a positive way? Walking in your purpose you can. Do not doubt yourself. There should be a sense of excitement brewing up inside of you to do better, making you want to align yourself more in your assigned purpose.

I pray these words of encouragement inspired and uplifted you to awaken the purpose inside of you. Do not allow anything—not even your own self to stop you. Life comes with tests and trials; you make a difference when you keep going forward. There is no age range when you can discover your purpose. Purpose and passion are for the young and old.

Power in Prayer

Dear God,

I thank you for your grace and mercy. God, please touch the person reading this book. Give them guidance and direction. Help them understand their fully assigned purpose. Help them to allow and trust the process you have for their life. Comfort them when things seem overwhelming. Relax them when life gets agitated. May your will be done in their life. God, I pray the person reading this prayer gets a hunger for their assigned purpose. Cover them in the blood of Jesus. God, we thank you now.

Amen!

Be encouraged!

Nuggets of Purpose

Ronjeanna's Encouraging Writings

Things to consider when it comes to Purpose!

- ➢ Recognize Distraction.
- ➢ The enemy hears your declarations unto God.
- ➢ Take Notice of the tactics of the devil.
- ➢ You must study the bible for clarity.
- ➢ You must stay prayed up.
- ➢ Let God clean up the mess in you.
- ➢ Deal with the bed you have made.
- ➢ Learn to be fully obedient to the voice of God.
- ➢ Give everything to God: your life and others depend on it.
- ➢ Stay on track.
- ➢ God is fixing and shaping you.
- ➢ Let God be the Architect.

Positive Quotes

- *It does not make a difference if you do not make a difference.*

- *I am determined to be greater.*

- *I have people purpose activation depending on my purpose execution.*

- *Become unrecognizable to the enemy by being attentive to God's directions.*

- *Be willing to go beyond the limit's life will try to set for you, mastering the indescribable that is assigned purpose.*

- *I dare you to Conquer and Win!*

- *I dare you to Soar and Make a Difference!*

- *I dare you to Inspire and Impact!*

- *I dare you to Embrace your Journey with Confidence!*

www.ingramcontent.com/pod-product-compliance
Lightning Source LLC
LaVergne TN
LVHW051210080426
835512LV00019B/3197